STORIES TO TELL

An easy guide to self publishing
family history books & memoirs

by Nancy Barnes

www.StoriesToTellBooks.com ‖ 888-577-9342

History will be kind to me, for I intend to write it.
~Sir Winston Churchill

CONTENTS

PART 1 IMAGINE

PART 2 PLAN

PART 3 CREATE

PART 4 EDIT

PART 5 DESIGN

PART 6 PUBLISH

INTRODUCTION

Are your stories important? Absolutely! We tell stories to make sense of our lives, to remember important events and to pass on what we know to others. Whether your stories are about your personal triumphs and trials, about your family's history, or dedicated to memories of loved ones - we all have good reasons for telling stories.

Imagine yourself as a journalist who has traveled to a foreign country, and returned to write about what you experienced. Your book is a document of social history, describing real people's lives, to transmit to future generations.

More important, your book is a document of your own personal and family history. When extended families lived closely together, these stories might have been told repeatedly around the dinner table. Today, our young people may not have the opportunity to truly listen. When they become older, with children of their own, they will wish they had asked more questions of you. We've all experienced those regrets. Imagine, your book might be a revelation to a descendant you haven't met yet!

Children yearn to understand the family they belong to, and your stories can give their lives meaning. Every family has stories that define the best part of who they are as a group. The hard-earned knowledge, experience and wisdom that you've gathered over the years is invaluable. How tragic if these precious memories were lost! Your stories should be passed on. Your family and friends will admire your efforts now, and they will value your book as a family treasure later.

Authors repeatedly tell us that creating a book is one of the most interesting, rewarding activities they've ever done. Why? Choosing which stories to tell and sorting through photos is an opportunity to examine your life, and to re-examine memories you haven't visited in years. You may find yourself on a more meaningful journey than you expected.

Preservation: Books are Still the Best Media

What about ebooks? How about that digital camcorder footage from the last family vacation? Perhaps these are enough to tell your stories, and you can be spared the trouble of writing a book.

Unfortunately, none of these technologies are reliable over time. After all, whatever happened to those VHS movies? The Library of Congress, as well as other digital media experts, still advises us to document history on paper. Books can last for hundreds of years. (CD's are not reliable beyond two years, so back up your data!) Ironically, the lasting value of books is because they are "low tech" and don't require a machine to operate.

That doesn't mean that a multimedia presentation isn't engaging and valuable. Consider supplementing your book with a companion CD that holds all the photos you've published, and more that didn't make it into the book. It is also easy to create a companion ebook to accompany your book. Ask your editor or book designer how you can coordinate the two projects.

Why an Illustrated Book?

The world of books is changing, and for the better. Printing technologies make it possible to include pictures throughout a book relatively inexpensively. In the old days, those few precious color plates were grouped together, with the bulk of the book being text. Don't we all go directly to the pictures?

If you recall the pleasure of reading children's books, you know how powerful illustrations can be. This is not just for children anymore. Graphic novels are being produced for readers of all ages. Readers, especially the readers of the future, are changing. The possibilities for sharing images, as well as words, make books that much more valuable.

However, this movement toward images does not devalue the written word or the power of the story. For example, think of those family photo albums, the ones that contain pictures without names or stories to explain them. If you have ever puzzled through such an album, you know how little a picture conveys without a story to expain it. The knowledge of the storyteller is invaluable.

Memoirs and Family Histories: Literary Cousins

Why don't you ever see a family history section in a library or bookstore? Because they are included among the memoirs. In fact, memoirists often include family history in their books, but provide the historical information from their current point of view.

Another reason family histories are rarely seen in these public venues is because they are often considered of limited interest to anyone but the family. In fact, if you wish, you can write a commercially compelling family history to appeal to a broad audience. How? Write it like a memoir.

Memoirists use the methods of fiction and literature to craft their books. A memoir need not be an attempt to document your entire life. In fact a lot of people are better off focusing on a single aspect of their lives, a time period or experience. The idea of a memoir is to deal with the feelings and emotions a particular time or event engendered. You can hold that experience up, examine it and see what insights may be drawn from it.

Rather than slogging through all the days of your life, you can select a more limited focus:

- Your experiences raising children
- Your military career
- Memories of childhood or adolescence
- Travel memories
- Overcoming an obstacle or illness
- An important relationship

In a memoir of this sort you can focus on more personal details, emotions and insights as well as inspirational or humorous moments than you can when trying to cover the scope of your entire life. This focus can quickly eliminate the frustrations of trying to find something to say about periods of your life that seem less interesting. If you decide to write about the things you find more interesting or inspirational or which gave you the most important insights, the chances are your reader will appreciate it.

Types of Family History Books

When you set out to create a family history book you have a lot of options. There is no fixed model for what a family history should look like; it is a matter of personal preference. The choice may be determined by the family artifacts you want to preserve, or the availability of stories you want to include. Here are a few common types:

Pure genealogy, combining pedigree charts, family group sheets and other forms to document the family's vital records.

Photo books, which trace the family history through photographs, providing biographical information of ancestors and details of events in photo captions.

Collections of letters and documents, which then provide details in brief notes, much as captions do with photo books.

Family cookbooks recording favorite recipes, often interspersed with stories.

Family diaries or journals usually speak for themselves, and require little more than transcription with an occasional explanatory detail.

The two forms that we favor most are, not surprisingly, story intensive. We prefer them because we feel they will be more interesting and valuable to readers. Both take a more literary, dramatic, and thematic approach and have beeen used by successful commercial authors.

The first, a combined memoir and family narrative, usually goes back just a generation or two and summarizes the lives of family members. However, the focus is primarily on the author's own dramatic experiences. The past generations are part of the story because of their role in the narrator's life.

Family narratives tell family stories over multiple generations. They use judicious speculation to "characterize" distant ancestors. These books often effectively combine features like photos, documents, letters, and recipes to enhance the narrative.

The Author's Journey

Writing a family history or memoir can be an extraordinary creative experience. Creating your book is an opportunity for personal exploration and self-discovery. You will have the opportunity to tell your stories, your way. The book you produce will be as unique as the people whose history is its subject.

That being said, the prospect of embarking on an unknown journey can be intimidating. Some people spend years gathering their research without getting to the draft stage of the book. We've all seen the cliché of the brilliant artist struck by inspiration. However, that's not how most of us create. As writing teachers and editors, we know that the process of writing a book can be broken down into simple steps that most everyone can follow. Instead of thinking of creating a book as an art, think of it as a craft.

We have broken down the process of creating a book, start to finish, into six simple steps. Follow them as you would follow a cookbook recipe. First you will gather your ingredients, then prepare them, then serve the finished product. If you are willing to read the recipe and to experiment with a new experience, there is no reason you cannot craft a book!

This book is divided into six steps to guide you through the process with helpful exercises. We suggest reading this book first before going ahead with your project. It is easier to take a journey when you've looked at the map!

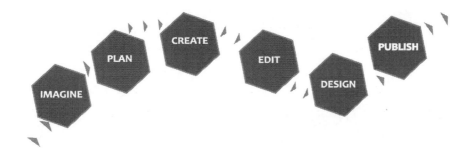

1. Imagine

Sort through your memories, photos and documents. Do the exercises in Part 1 of this guide to get a variety of ideas.

2. Plan

Plan the order of your stories. Use the charts in Part 2, and arrange stories on your outline. Use a photo binder to organize your images.

3. Create

Create your text by writing or by recording stories, and then having the recording transcribed. Scan your photos, or have your book designer scan them. Give both text and photos to your editor.

4. Edit

Your editor creates a manuscript from your materials, both editing and correcting the content. You'll examine the manuscript, and then confer with your editor to determine any changes you'd like.

5. Design

Your book is designed, both interior and cover. Photos are placed; text is laid out, your cover is designed. You confer with your designer to determine what you want it to look like. You then receive a final proof copy for approval.

6. Publish

Choose the right printer or publisher, depending on the goals for your book. When the book design is perfect, it is sent to the printer of your choice. You may wish to order in bulk, or order a few at a time from an online bookstore.

PART 1
IMAGINE

First, Overcome Your Obstacles

Creating a book doesn't happen in a day. It is a long-term project, and it takes conviction, some effort, and positive thinking to get it done.

There are good reasons (and many excuses) why people don't succeed at completing their book. Let's begin by eliminating the most common obstacles with practical solutions.

1. Time

Time is a precious, limited commodity, and there are always other things to do. You can procrastinate for years, as no one else but you will demand that you complete your book. The answer? In the short term, you should allot time to this project as your most important hobby time, just as you would allow time for other passionate, enjoyable pursuits in your life. Some other hobby must give way– TV viewing, perhaps?

In the long term, you need to calendar out the project. Plan backwards. Set a reasonable date in the future, generally from 4 months to 2 years, depending on how much you've done so far. For example, I might plan to have the book done for my birthday, or for the family reunion next summer. Then plan how to get everything done before then. Allow the most time for the earlier steps of imagining, planning and creating your draft. The final three steps are done by professionals relatively quickly, perhaps in 6 weeks to 3 months, depending on your circumstances.

Share your calendar regularly with family and friends, so that they support you and keep you motivated both as you work on the book and on your long-term goal of finishing it.

2. Organization

We can become overwhelmed with choices when we have too many stories, and too many photos and documents. The solution? Use an organizational plan and stick to it. Everything that doesn't fit into the plan for your book can be used in a different book later, or archived on a CD, if preservation is your goal.

These are skills you learned in school – remember those reports you wrote, and the outline you used? Fortunately, the adult mind is much more capable of logical organization than when we were children! Part 2 has charts you can use to get organized.

3. Writing

Not everyone has a talent for writing, and even experienced writers dread staring at a blank page. The phrase "write a book" can paralyze a beginning author. How to overcome this obstacle? First of all, divide your outline into manageable chunks, and sit down at regular intervals to produce a story at a time. If you enjoy writing, this is a natural "session", so you'll simply type until you've told that story.

If you do not enjoy writing, then fall back on your more-developed skill, speaking. We are all skilled at spoken language, and more experienced with communicating stories in our own voice. You can buy an inexpensive hand held recorder, or record directly on to your computer. The recording can be transcribed, fairly inexpensively, saving you the trauma of trying to write your book! You will be amazed at how many pages speech generates. We talk much faster than we can type. You can speak in a very relaxed manner, knowing you can always fix it later.

Use the transcription as a rough draft, and modify anything you said that was inaccurate. You can add artful touches, if you like. Once you have the rough draft, you'll find you are more comfortable with "writing" your book.

4. Cost

Self publishing costs money. Even if you intend to market your book, you are unlikely to find a publisher willing to give you an advance on sales. However, it doesn't have to cost a lot to self publish, and often the fear of the unknown leads people to imagine the worst.

You can control your expenses in several ways. The biggest is to choose the correct printer or publisher for your project. Many people overspend because they do not know their way around the publishing industry. Don't pay for services, such as marketing packages, that you don't need, and don't pay for extra books that you don't need.

What do you need to spend on? It depends on your skills, your technological competence, and whether you want the convenience of someone to help you. If you own a scanner and are skilled in Photoshop, this can save you money. If you have a friend who is a professional editor, this can save you money. If you already own and use book design software, this can save you money. You can print a "do it yourself" book at the local copy shop, if you don't care about the quality of the book.

To produce a professional book, even an experienced author turns to professionals. You will generally need an editor and a book designer, and often one or both will advise you about a good printer or publisher you can work with.

If you have your manuscript truly "done", and your images are truly prepared correctly, then you will require minimal services from your editor and designer. The cost of getting published then is dictated by the length of the book, as editors and designers and book printers charge by quantity, such as the number of pages and images. However, don't let this limit the scope of your project. If you are creating a big, wonderful book, you'll face these service fees just once, but your book will live forever!

Three Big Questions

Take a few minutes to reflect upon three questions before embarking on your book. The answers you choose can guide you toward the type of stories and images you should include.

1. Which type of book is for you? Fast and easy, or slow and thoughtful?

Fast and easy: You don't have a lot of material in mind, and you want a shorter book in a short time. You just want to get your stories down on paper. You would be happy to follow easy instructions, if only someone would help you to get this book done.

Slow and thoughtful: You don't have a deadline. You want to reflect, compose thoughtfully, and savor the creative experience of authorship. You'll invest time on this project to create a lengthy, complex book.

If you're the "fast and easy" type, we recommend following this guide very literally. Choose one of the formulas for organizing stories, and stick to it. Once you have your rough draft completed, tell your editor you're in a hurry, and to "micro edit"- don't make major revisions. It will speed you toward publication.

Why take more time to create your book when you can finish faster? Because creating a book can be a highly creative, very enjoyable process. Sorting through memories, or family history research, documents and old photographs is a wonderful opportunity for reflection. You may wish to read a few books on writing, join a writing group, and explore some literary possibilities before committing to the outline of your stories.

2. What are your goals?

☑ To successfully complete a wonderful book

❐ To review my own life or family history, in order to understand it better

❐ To pass on family stories or my own story to future generations

❐ To leave a historical account of the times I have lived through

❐ To enjoy reminiscing and reliving the good times

❐ To give an honest account of my own life

❐ To make my mark by describing my challenges and achievements

❐ To publish my memoir for a general commercial audience

❐ Other

3. Who is your audience?

Consider how you answered the questions about goals and now relate them to your audience. After all, this book is for you, first, since you're the one who will live with it as a project. If no one else ever reads it, then how would you write it, as the sole audience?

Second, after your enjoyment, should be consideration of the people you are doing this for. Your audience helps you to shape, and perhaps censor, the content.

Exercise: Consider the following passage, and then write a brief description of your audience – your relationship, their interests, and what you want to tell them.

Who do you intend to read your book? Consider your book a direct communication, as the people who already know you will get to know you better. If you are you speaking to children/ grandchildren, consider what they want and need to know. Imagine the unborn child who is fascinated by family history – what will you leave for that special child?

In contrast, if you're writing for an adult audience, your style and story choices will differ. Who are the adults who will read your book? How will they react? What might they desire to contribute or to see preserved? Considering this makes it easier for you to narrow or broaden your choice of stories.

File everything. *If there isn't an appropriate folder, name a new one. Notes on odd sized scraps of paper can be taped to 8 ½" X 11" paper before filing – they will be much easier to flip through later. Give a title and date to every note. If your notes on a topic run to multiple pages, number and staple them together before filing.*

You will find that you have ideas and flashes of memory at odd times, not only when you're working on your book. The trick is to capture these thoughts and jot them down as they occur to you.

Get Organized Now, Before You Start

The exercises in the next chapter will create a mess of paper – notes, lists, photos, maybe even drawings – often called "brainstorming". You'll need a system to keep your notes and the project in order. With your files in order, you'll feel more in control of where you're going with the book. And, if you do this now, great ideas won't get lost in the shuffle!

Use manila folders to create files; or use computer folders. (You'll still need to organize papers, though.) Files you will need:

- Brainstorming Ideas
- Good Story Ideas
- Stories That Go Together
- Themes/Topics
- A Folder for each chapter (Chapter #1, #2, etc.)
- Facts to Check
- Quotations
- Photographs
- Documents
- Interviews
- Potential Chapter Titles
- Questions to be Answered
- Correspondence

Brainstorming

To brainstorm is to generate ideas rapidly, without any attempt to shape or direct the creative process. The idea is to list many ideas, good and bad, and to sort them out later. Remember, "more is better". This section contains many exercises to get you started. This process can take days or even weeks – it's up to you to decide when you have enough good story ideas to make a book.

Sorting Photographs For Stories

They say that every picture tells a story. Well, some do, at least. Your photographs can serve several purposes: to remind you of stories you want to tell, to suggest categories of stories to include, or perhaps to illustrate your book. Not all of your photos are good enough to go into a book. But for now, use all of them for ideas.

Look through your photographs quickly and sort them into two piles: story and no story. (Puzzling out those unknown landscapes and forgotten acquaintances can be distracting!)

Take time with each of your "yes, they do have a story" photos. Try to answer the Journalist's Questions (who, what, when, where, why, and how) for each photograph. Take notes.

Allow yourself to return to the era in each picture. Recall the background as well as the foreground of that time; what was happening behind the scenes with family or friends? What the camera didn't capture is part of the story, even though it may not be part of the photo. Take notes.

After you've done this exercise, keep your better photographs, the ones that are candidates for use in the book, in your photographs folder. You'll want to sort through them again after you have selected the stories you will tell.

File your notes with the photographs in your "Photographs" folder. Handle the prints with care – don't write on the backs or stick notes on them.

Do Your Images Lead Your Stories?

Now that you've looked at your photos, there is a fork in the road; there are two ways to proceed. Ask yourself, "Do I want my images to be the primary organizing principle to guide the narrative, or do the stories come first, with images supplementing my stories?"

Imagine *Life Magazine*. It's a form of story telling, pictorial history. Vivid pictures are used to tell a story, and text is used to supplement and explain the images.

To create a pictorial history, choose images first, and eliminate stories that are not tied directly to illustrations. (We'll discuss using images other than photos in "Sorting Documents" next.)

When choosing your photographs, consider:

1. The physical quality of the images. Are the photos faded, torn, scratched?

2. The vividness of the story told by the photograph. Is it interesting enough?

Choose photographs that:

- Evoke laughter or cause emotion

- Are candid and show character

- Show stages of life; such as pictures of the same person taken years apart

- Are action shots; in general they're more interesting than posed photos

- Are close-ups rather than long distance shots

- Are more horizontal than vertical; these usually make better illustrations

Image Quality

Use good or excellent photos to illustrate your book. However, you may choose to include a photo of lesser quality if it is rare or important. If so, have the image restored or retouched.

Unacceptable Quality

Poor Quality

Unacceptable: Very faded, little contrast, will be of poor quality even with photo restoration.
Poor: Has some intact image, but damage must be cropped out, may be retouched to "fair".

Good Quality

Excellent Quality

Good: Clear image, color and contrast can be easily adjusted
Excellent: High resolution images from digital cameras and pro photographers need no work.

Sorting Documents

Many families have treasure troves of documents stashed away in the attic, for "later". This may be the right time! Many documents tell an important story about your family's history. Even if you don't know the story, including a copy in your book is a good way to preserve historical documents. Some documents you might consider:

- birth and baptismal certificates, family Bibles, family trees

- death notices, obituaries, funeral programs, cemetery records, headstone inscriptions

- naturalization and citizenship papers

- property deeds, mortgage records

- school records, diplomas, transcripts, report cards, yearbooks

- marriage and divorce records

- wills and estate papers

- military records

- scrapbooks

- journals or diaries / old letters

- adoption or guardianship records

Linden N. J.
Dec 19–43

Dear Joe.

We didn't hear from you much lately; hoping you don't let the parting of your two pals get you down Did you hear from them yet and if you did let us know if they came up our way.

I asked you several time who your chaplain is but

Oversized documents and small items can be scanned. If you have precious or fragile items, it is better to take them to a local scanning service rather than sending them in the mail. Have the local scanning service e-mail the digital files to your book designer.

Top Ten Lists

In fact, there is nothing magical about the number 10. Your lists may have 7 or 12 items on a list– whatever works for you.

Exercise: For each topic, create your list on a separate sheet of paper. Title and date it. After you've done your lists, consider which item has a good story(s) associated with it. Then highlight or underline those lines. They may be the stories worth using in your book.

Too overwhelming? Too much work? Then try this.

Consider your book goals. Then read the list of topics. Put an X next to just 3 topics, the ones most relevant for your book idea. Then consider only your most often told, favorite, sure-to-please stories that fit those topics.

- the ten most important turning points in your life

- the ten family stories you would like to see preserved

- the most influential people in your life (note a sentence or two about how each influenced you)

- your greatest disappointments

- your core values: consider how these are illustrated by events in your life

- areas in which you might have been considered an expert

- your best friends

- as many humorous stories in your or your family's life as you can remember

- hobbies or activities that have been important to you

- childhood events that still seem important to you

- ten things you value most in your life

- all the places to which you have travelled

- your greatest accomplishments

- your regrets

- your happiest moments

- your recurring dreams

Chronological Stages of Life

Create your own custom "stages of life" chart on a sheet of lined paper or in a word processing document. (You may have to modify the stages we have listed to reflect your life, or the life of your subject, more accurately.) Leave room on your chart for a list of events that occurred at each stage.

Stages	Events
Birth / Infancy	1. 2. (Number each section with as many stories as you wish to include.) 3.
Preschool Years	1.
Elementary School Years	1. 2.
Teen Years	
Young Adult Years	
Early Career Years	
Middle Career Years	
Late Career Years	
Retirement	

A Life Resume

Consider these topics for yourself and/or for others you may write about. Select three (or more) that you find most interesting and relevant. For each topic, create a list on a separate sheet of paper and brainstorm about them, taking notes. After you've done all five lists, consider which entries have a good story or stories associated with them. Highlight or mark those lines, indicating you may wish to use them in your book.

All of these topics will also apply to family history book planning. These personal elements, if the details are known, are an invaluable record of social history. They will bring the interests and preoccupations of your ancestors to life. Consider developing a life resume for each of the ancestors featured in your book.

Work Experience

Include jobs from your first to your most recent. Reflect on successes, failures, disappointments, lessons learned and memorable experiences associated with each one.

Relationships

This might include family relationships, friends, lovers, even rivals or antagonists. What was your role in each relationship? How did you grow in them? What did you learn from each one?

Health History

How did health influence your life? Did you have accidents or major illnesses to overcome? How did these experiences shape you?

Places You Have Lived

Where and with whom have you lived? Recall the highlights of the time you lived there. What do you recall about the place itself?

Travel

Try to list all the places you have visited. Think of the highlights of those trips. Who did you meet? What did you learn?

Hobbies

What pastimes have been special to you? Why?

Favorites

Books, music, movies, foods, clothes, cars, etc. Why did you find each of them memorable?

Lessons

Have you gained any insights about life? What are they? How did you learn those lessons?

Successes

What goals have you achieved? What obstacles have you overcome?

Failures

On what goals have you fallen short? What lessons did you learn from the experience? What did you do instead?

Your Place in History

This exercise can provide some broader social/political/historical context for your stories. Although you may not have participated directly in major historical events, they probably have impacted you and your family in important ways. If you're writing for an audience who are not of the same generation, some context will help them to understand the place and time.

Draw a line down the center of a piece of paper to create a chart like the one shown below.

FIRSTS	CURRENT EVENTS
On this side of the chart list important firsts in your life. Examples: first day of school, first best friend, first love, first failure, first career, first home owned, first child, first long trip, etc.	On this side, list events that were making news about the time of your first. The events may be historic or cultural. (Examples: The Korean War, the McCarthy Hearings, the Cuban Missile Crisis, the Beatles' Appearance on the Ed Sullivan Show, the first moon landing, the gas lines of the 1970s, the premier of Star Wars, the First Gulf War, etc.

This method of placing individual's lives in the context of history is especially useful if your family stories are incomplete. You can safely speculate about what an ancestor's life was like by exploring their place and time.

References to larger social and cultural issues can also give your stories depth and symbolic meaning beyond just personal experience.

Spatial Memory: Drawing to Recall Places

This is a fun exercise. Draw a floor plan of a house where you once lived. Label all the rooms. Put in any details about the rooms you can remember. Make sure to note any memories that the floor plan brings back as you draw it.

Draw a map of a neighborhood in which you lived. Label the streets. Mark the location of the buildings you recall. What people lived or worked in those buildings? Take your time and put in as much detail as you can. Make notes on anything the map helps you recall as you draw it.

Visual Imagination: My Life as a Movie

Are you the type who thinks in pictures? If you're a visual learner, here's the perfect exercise for you.

Imagine you are a director in Hollywood, and you have been hired to make a movie - of your own life. Your film must be limited to only two hours of screen time, so you must identify only the most important elements of the life it will portray.

As you know, movies often jump from scene to scene, and in some films the scenes are not in chronological order. This can also be true of books.

On a blank piece of paper, list ten to twenty "scenes" from your life that you think are essential to the movie. Try reordering them a few times for the best cinematic effect.

Verbal Brainstorming: Interviewing Family and Friends

This can be a very enjoyable, affirming exercise. If nothing else, it's an excuse to catch up with your family and old friends to reminisce. Our authors are often happily surprised that their loved ones have been listening very closely to them all along!

List up to ten of your closest family and friends. Try to select people whom you have known for a long time, and people you have trusted and confided in most over the years.

Call or visit them. Allow time for a lengthy conversation, and make sure they have free time, too.

Explain that you're working on a book, and trying to sort out what stories of are most interesting and entertaining.

Ask them what their stories about you and/or your family are. What does your friend think is the most important thing about you, the thing that makes you unique? What would they tell others about you, if they were going to introduce you?

Ask them what stories you've told them, over time, that have stayed with them. Ask, "What's the best story I ever told you?" (Often they'll be your favorites, too.)

Thank them, and tell them you'll keep them updated on the project. They'll often think about it more and call you with more ideas.

Take good notes, or better yet, record your conversation.

Stories to Keep, Stories to Eliminate

Brainstorming is fun. Once you start remembering stories, it's hard to stop! But brainstorming is also uncritical – it mixes the good with the bad. Before you go on to the next step, consider the stories that should perhaps be eliminated.

Your life and history most likely has its traumatic moments and dark secrets. They may feel uncomfortable or difficult to talk about. Do you have to include them in your book? No. Should you? How much "truth" should you tell?

One way to make the decision is to imagine every person who will read your book. Would you be comfortable revealing the information to them, face to face? Do you want to? If not, just don't include it. Consider these questions before revealing painful truths.

- Is the truth necessary to tell your larger story?

- Will the story hurt anyone if you bring it out into the open?

- Was it common knowledge at the time it happened?

- Does it deliberately vilify someone? Does your telling of the story show malice or spite?

- Is it fair to all concerned?

- Are you telling the story only for its sensational value?

- Are people in the story still alive? Can you talk to them about it?

- How will it affect any children involved?

- What will be gained if you include it?

- What will be lost if you omit it from your book?

If You Can't Quite Remember, Exactly

You will probably find that despite your best efforts there are stories that you remember only partially, or not at all.

One thing you can do you to recall the parts you can't remember is to write about the parts you can recall. Write, talk, and reminisce about the general times, people, and places surrounding your lost memory. Things you have forgotten pop into your consciousness – see? You had them all along - and they can be added to the story.

A conversation, in person or by telephone, with a family member or old friend is a great way to help yourself to recall partially remembered stories. Talking about your shared memories will bring back details of stories you may have forgotten, or trigger memories you have completely forgotten.

If you have tried, and you still can't quite grasp the memory, then what do you do? Leave it out. Admit that you can't remember and move on. You can't tell everything, not even all of what you remember fully. Writing a memoir is a process of choosing what to include and what to leave out. Leaving something out because you can't remember enough details to tell the story well is a good decision.

Speculation in Family History

What's the level of truth or historical accuracy required of the author of a family history? It's a question almost guaranteed to come up in a conversation with a person working on a family history book.

Two basic concerns lie behind the question. First, people are worried about faulty memories – their own or particularly those of elderly relatives they may interview. Do they remember correctly? Second, the further one moves back in time, the more likely it is that there are gaps in the factual record of the person or people you are writing about. What if you can't find the facts?

The firestorms over the false memoir James Frey created and fictional journalism of people like Jayson Blair demonstrate that almost no one thinks it's okay to simply make things up. But when you can't get at the facts, can you speculate about what happened? That's a trickier question.

Perhaps the answer ultimately comes down to the effort you've made to learn as much as you can. If you are relying primarily on interviews, have you talked to everyone you can who might help set the record straight? Have you done research to fill in the gaps? Examining the social history of the time and place you're writing about can give you insights into how people like the one you are writing about lived. Local historical societies can be particularly helpful. But no matter what you do, you probably won't answer every question you wish you could have.

When you have done as much as you think you can, you have to speculate to tell your story. That's what historians do. They learn as much as they can from the factual record, then draw a conclusion about what happened.

Journalist, critic and fiction writer Tom Bissell put it well when he said, "What the memoirist [or family historian] owes the reader is the ability to persuade that the narrator is trying, as honestly as possible, to get to the bottom of the experience at hand."

PART 2
PLAN

Organizing the Contents of Your Book

If you've done some or all of the exercises in the previous section, you have many stories, photos, and perhaps documents you want to include in your book. It is possible to simply choose your favorites and present them as a "short story collection" – short story writers do that all the time. If you're in a hurry, this is an easy option.

However, your readers will understand your book better if the stories are gathered into clearly identified chapters. There are no hard-and-fast-rules about how to organize chapters. Generally, they fall into two broad organizational categories: chronological or topical. These are not mutually exclusive methods. You can use a chronological structure, and then include topical stories. An example: "1968-1974: My Changing Views About War."

One way to begin organizing is to choose a type of memoir or family history; then the logical structure will follow. As you read the descriptions on the following page, consider whether your stories fit into any of these categories. If not, how would you describe your book's organization?

Chronological Memoir or Family History

The stories of one person's life, from childhood to the time of writing, including the person's experience with previous generations of the family. Unlike autobiography, chronological memoir is selective; key dramatic stories reveal the author's experiences, feelings, and interpretations, often those shaping character over the course of a lifetime (or generations).

Collection of Stories On One Topic

These stories are about a topic you've had a long and extensive experience with. For example, a chef writes a memoir about his life in the kitchen, or a well traveled writer tells stories about trips to foreign lands.

Collection of Stories About Related Topics or Themes

A broader range of stories grouped under a large topical umbrella to provide some organization to the book as a whole. For example, A book titled "Emotions" permits one or more chapters about any and all sorts of emotions. The stories might be only loosely related, but the broad theme allows the author more freedom to include disparate stories.

A Specific Chapter in Your Life

These books focus upon a specific time or theme in your life. It might be overcoming an illness, a personal achievement, an account of your travels, or military experience.

Family History

These books are primarily designed to preserve family history, and so must be more fact-based, and may be less concerned with entertaining the reader. They are often ordered chronologically, and should include as many family documents, records and artifacts as possible. (We discussed varieties of family histories in the Introduction.)

Biographical Profiles

For family historians, this method of organization is based on the individuals who comprise your family history. Profiles can be grouped by generation, or by the branch of the family. This organization is effective when you have varied material, as one person's profile might include photos and developed stories, while a more distant ancestor's section might only contain a brief summary of facts you have gathered with a few accompanying documents.

Tribute to a Loved One or a Relationship

These books honor someone else's admirable character traits and achievements. You can include both first-hand stories of your times together, and second-hand stories as well, so that you can give a fuller history of the person.

Transmission of Personal, Ethical or Religious Values

This type of book is sometimes called an "ethical will" - a collection of instructions for how to live, a discussion of your personal or religious values, and important family stories that you seek to pass on to children or grandchildren. The stories are more instructive than simply entertaining.

Other

If you are thinking of creating a very different book than the examples above, try to describe it in a summary like the above to clarify your purpose.

The Scope of Your Book

Consider the scale, or scope of your book. How much time does it span? How many "characters" does it contain? Generally, the distant past has fewer stories, and you may need to speculate more about the unknown. Current experience has the opposite challenge: too much material.

The goal is to include stories with depth and meaning throughout your book. If you lack content for an era, skip it, or simply present images and move on to more interesting stories.

1 ⟶
Documentation of distant past : spanning 4+ generations
Broad & shallow content: some facts, few images, few stories
(many story details must be inferred)

2 ⟶
Recent history : spans 2 or 3 generations
Has more facts, more varied images. The author can recall
retold stories and paraphrase them, and include some
current generation stories.

3 ⟶
Living memory: stories are recalled firsthand. They may
include family history, but only in the context of living
characters of the present generation (memoir).
Deeper content: the author must choose from (too?)
many facts, images & stories and use the best material.

You'll Need Working Titles

Working titles are an essential part of the logical organizational process. It eliminates much confusion when you give simple names to each of your chapters (and then again to your stories). Authors call them "working titles". They indicate the one essential organizing principle of the chapter or story.

Use this formula to compose a working title: Who, Where, When. Every story has them. When you have two stories about the same person, refine the place and/or time. Example: Tony's House, Brooklyn 1978. Two stories? June 1978, August 1978. You'll know exactly which story you're referring to.

Some authors want to number chapters 1, 2, 3, etc. We find this causes big problems. You need to know what goes into each chapter and why. The working titles will remind you, and your editor, of your plan. So, before you begin to write or record your stories, assign working titles to your stories and chapters. You and your editor can understand one another by referring to working titles when you discuss the draft.

Later, when your rough draft is completed, and together with your editor you have "locked down" the final form of your manuscript, you can read each chapter and compose a fitting title, or opt to keep your working title, or opt not to title your chapters at all.

Chronological Chapter Organization

The majority of memoirs rely on the deceptively simple approach of describing events in the order they occurred. However, don't let "What happened next?" dictate the contents of your book. You should not expect to give equal attention to each period in your life. Instead, ask yourself, "What are the most important events?" The bulk of the book should be devoted to these important events.

Chapters in a chronologically organized book are created around periods of time. The sample chart on the upcoming page gives general guidelines. They can be easily adapted to any life story.

Some chronological chapters deal with longer periods of years; a decade may be covered in a quick summary. Other chapters may cover shorter times and examine them in greater depth. For example, you might deal with your childhood, high school, and college in just one short chapter, and then devote a long, full chapter to that single critical year that you began your career.

In the same way, in a family history, some periods are developed more than others. American families are fascinated with the details of their immigration to the United States. Less critical in this context is a description of a corporate career, as this is familiar ground.

If you are going to organize your book chronologically, recreate the following chart, customizing the ages, dates, and phases to accurately reflect your book's stories.

Chronological Chapter Planning Chart

Chapter	My Age	Years	Phase of Your Life / Working Title
1	First 5 years	1937-1942	Birth and Childhood
2	5-13	1943-1950	Elementary School Years
3	13-19	1951-1956	Teen Years
4	20-25	1957-1962	Young Adult Years
5	26-35	1963-1972	Early Career Years
6	36-45	1973-1982	Early Middle Years
7	46-55	19823-1992	Later Middle Years
8	56-65	1993-2002	Late Career Years
9	65+	2002+	Retirement Years

Topical Chapter Organization

This method of organization can take as many forms as there are topics. In theory, your entire book might be a very specific topic, such as your relationship with your cat, but most of us fear that our readers won't find such a narrow topic entertaining. Therefore, memoirists tend to choose broader, more inspirational, thoughtful, dramatic or entertaining topics.

Topical Chapter Planning Chart - Themes for Family History

Topics	Working Title	Chapter
Good family times Beliefs Careers & Skills	Example Title: "Places We Lived 1663-1996" (Stories of the times and places our ancestors have moved.)	5
Hobbies Travels	Example Title: "A Family of Teachers" 5 generations 1896-2007	2
Child-rearing Places we've lived Achievements		
Important friends Disappointments Tragedies		
Foods / recipes Religion Dilemmas / choices		
Social changes Historic changes		

Topical Chapter Planning Chart - Themes for Memoir

My Topics	My Working Title	Chapter#
Good family times Career	**Example**: my title is "I've Moved Around" (I'll combine all the places I have lived.)	5
Hobbies Travels		
Child-rearing Places I've lived		
Achievements Best friends		
Disappointments Lessons learned		
Tragedies Wisdom earned		
Memories of my child Memories of my spouse		
Memories of my parents		
Memories of my siblings		
Favorite foods / recipes Beliefs		
Religion Dilemmas / choices		
Personal changes Social changes		
Historic changes		

Ideas for Topical Organization

Turning Points

Focus each chapter on key situations or events that changed your life. These are often dramatic, interesting stories to tell. Be sure to describe what happened in full detail, and explain why it is important to you.

Personal Themes

Organize the chapters around the different elements of your life. Chapters can be organized by topics such as Family Times, Friends, Career, Hobbies, Travels, etc.

Character Traits

This method of organization is particularly useful if you are writing a tribute book. When you are telling someone else's story, you can single out their positive character traits. (If the book is about you, the positive character traits might seem like bragging.) Consider chapters such as Courage, Intelligence, Sense of Humor, Creativity, or Persistence.

Values

If your purpose in writing a your book is to focus on cultural or spiritual values, organize your chapters around the values demonstrated in your stories. Some positive values: Faith, Loyalty, Commitment, Honor, Compassion, Respect, and Forgiveness. Use chapter introductions and conclusions to talk about the meaning of each value, in addition to telling your stories.

Accomplishments

Whether they are personal accomplishments or successes in your career, memoirs that detail accomplishments also need to show conflict. For each story, describe the obstacles you had to overcome, so that it doesn't seem as though success came too easily!

Other

If you have a different topic, can you name it? Create one umbrella term for your chapter and stories fit under. If you can't, you may have stories that are "off topic" for your book. It's up to you whether to keep them, or to eliminate them for the sake of organization.

Put Stories Into Your Chapters

Congratulations! You've decided what your chapter titles will be. Now you can plan which of your stories fit into each chapter.

On the adjoining page is a planning chart that will get your chapters organized.

If you find that you have only one story for a chapter, it's not as complex as your other chapters. This makes for an awkward structure. Rethink your chapters, perhaps combining two into one.

If you have more than five longer stories, perhaps your chapter's subject is too broad and should be divided into two. Shorter chapters keep your book balanced and the reader moving forward.

1. Copy this chart onto a piece of lined paper, or even better, recreate it on your computer. You'll need one chart per chapter. Fill in the established working title for the chapter.

2. Now revisit your stories, and assign them to their chapters. You'll need to devise working titles for the stories, too. Jot a few notes to ensure you recognize the exact story.

3. Find or create your manila file folders for each chapter. This outline can be stapled inside the cover. It will serve as a guide as you gather your photographs and documents for the chapter.

Chapter # _____

Chapter Working Title _____

Time Period_____

Story #1 Working Title _____ Identify the story with a brief summary: When? Where? Who? What happened?
Story #2 Working Title _____ Identify the story with a brief summary: When? Where? Who? What happened?
Story #3 Working Title _____ Identify the story with a brief summary: When? Where? Who? What happened?
Story #4 Working Title _____ Identify the story with a brief summary: When? Where? Who? What happened?
Story #5 Working Title _____ Identify the story with a brief summary: When? Where? Who? What happened?
(Optional) Chapter Introduction What do you want the reader to know about this time period, in history, and/or in your life? Why have you included these stories in this chapter?
(Optional) Chapter Conclusion Why were the things that happened in this chapter important? What did they show about you? What lessons did you learn?

The Introductory Chapter

Would you like to include an introduction in your book? Some memoirs and family histories contain one, some don't. Some authors introduce their book in the beginning of the first story, and leave it at that.

An introductory chapter is often much shorter than the later chapters, since it does not contain stories. Don't worry that the introduction may seem short.

Titling the introduction is optional. Give your introduction a title or simply leave it titled "Introduction".

Developing an (Optional) Introductory Chapter

Because the introduction to a book is not a story you can tell from memory or research, it is better to plan carefully to communicate the meaning of what you are going to say.   Here are some ideas to suggest the content of your introduction:

Explain what you hope to accomplish by telling your story.

- Who is your audience? Explain to them why you are writing this book for them.

- Explain why you believe that your story is of interest and importance to your audience.

- Discuss some of the main ideas in the stories you are going to tell. Explain why you chose these stories.

- Discuss how you hope to affect your audience. Perhaps you hope to inspire them to have a different understanding of you, the past, of their own life, or even to change their actions.

An (Optional) Concluding Chapter

You should plan your conclusion only after you have planned your book. Once you know the scope of the stories, you will be able to speak about them more clearly. Many authors save their conclusion for the last revision of the book. Having some feedback from others and having gone through the book-creating process gives you a deeper understanding than when you are just starting out.

A title is optional. You may choose to give your conclusion a title or simply leave it titled "Conclusion". Concluding chapters tend to be much shorter than the book's stories. Don't worry that the conclusion may seem short. Here are some ideas of what to include:

Reflect upon the things you have talked about in the previous chapters. Attempt to give your readers a context for understanding them.

As you discuss the ideas of the book, you don't need to go into details. Since they have just read your stories, readers will know what you are referring to.

You may want to look back at your purpose for writing a memoir. (You may have discussed this in the introduction, if you wrote one. Revisiting that topic is always appropriate, if you have new insights.) In the conclusion, you may examine the way the stories you have told have achieved that purpose.

A Master Plan: One Overall Outline of Your Book

☑ You have your chapters figured out and titled.

☑ You have assigned stories to the chapters.

☑ You have given the stories working titles, too.

You will need the outlines that you have created for each chapter. Each lists the stories in that chapter, and their working titles.

Now you're ready to make your master plan, what we call the Master Outline. The Master Outline is very simple, but you must commit to it.

These are the stories that will comprise your book. When you are sure that you have the final version of this outline, you've "locked in" -then you can begin to write or record your stories. You'll still have a great deal of flexibility to tell the stories any way you like – but try not to change the plan.

If you must rethink the very structure of your book after you have begun, stop writing immediately! You may end up on a detour, creating a lot of unsuitable material. It is not unusual to reorganize your chapters and stories, after you have received your draft manuscript from your editor. So stick to your plan, as you can still make changes later.

Try not to write or record stories unless you will include them in your book. A lot of time and effort goes into typing and editing stories, so you don't want to throw them away. Worse, you become attached to them, having created them, and then may want to make use of them even though they don't belong.

Instead, this process is designed to work from a well thought-out plan and to get it (mostly) right the first time!

The Master Outline

On the following page is the Master Outline Form. It can be adapted for every possible type of book. There are more spaces than you'll need. This allows for the different kinds of books our authors write. Don't imagine yourself having to fill in all the blanks – you might end up with an 800 page book!

The average author may collect three to five stories in a chapter. We've left room for ten stories per chapter, just in case. Make as many copies of the Master Outline Form as you need, starting with one form per chapter. (if you have more stories in a chapter than ten, simply assign two sheets to that chapter.) Create a multi-page outline which reflects every chapter and story you have planned.

When you have completed your master outline, create a duplicate for others to check over, including your editor. This is an excellent time to get feedback.

Use the check boxes on your master copy to mark off the box each time you write or record a story. It's very rewarding, and a good way to see you're making progress!

Filling in the Master Outline

1. Refer to your individual chapter outlines, and simply transfer your plans to this form. Continue until you have copied all your chapter plans to the Master Outline.

2. For each chapter, check the box in the Chapter column and write in the chapter number and the working title.

3. Next, list each story in that chapter. Check the box in the Story column, fill in the story number and the working title of the story.

4. If you are planning to give chapter introductions and/or conclusions just title them Chapter, number, Introduction (or Conclusion).

Master Outline

Chapter	Story	Number	Working Title	Complete
☐	☐			☐
☐	☐			☐
☐	☐			☐
☐	☐			☐
☐	☐			☐
☐	☐			☐
☐	☐			☐
☐	☐			☐
☐	☐			☐
☐	☐			☐

PART 3
CREATE

The Raw Materials: Text and Images

Every book boils down to these two elements: text and images. Yet there are endless questions about how to create and format them. If you are skilled with a computer, preparing your text and images so that they are ready to go will save you some money when you submit them to your editor and book designer. However, they can be reformatted as needed.

Dealing With Handwritten Text

Not all of us have a manuscript ready to go on the computer. There are two ways to deal with handwritten text. If the author is simply not a typist, it is most affordable for the author to read their handwritten writing aloud into a digital recorder. A transcriptionist can work more quickly from audio than deciphering handwriting, and this saved time saves you money.

The other possibility for handwritten text is to preserve it "as is", so that your reader can view the material in the original handwriting. This is appropriate for original documents, but places a greater burden on the reader, who may not take the trouble. Consider accompanying images of handwritten documents and letters with a typed transcription, if the writing is at all unclear.

To Scan, or Not to Scan?

One of the most common hold-ups we experiences as book designers is poorly scanned images that are not acceptable for reproduction in a book. Many people own inexpensive "all in one" scanners, and are not aware of the correct software settings when they scan. These images look fine on a computer screen at low resolutions, but their flaws will show when printed in a book.

We will give specific instructions for scanning later in this chapter, but consider this general rule of thumb: if you are not experienced at scanning already, don't try to learn how on such an important project. It is better to give your originals to a professional shop, your editor or (best choice) your book designer, than to botch it and have to redo it later.

Should I Format My Book in Word?

We are often contacted by people who have already formatted their book, including illustrations, in Microsoft Word. This is really unfortunate. Printers usually don't work with books in Word format, and if they do, they are willing to produce sub-standard books. When you incorporate an image into Word, its quality is reduced, making it unusable for high quality printing. As for the text, a book designer will be removing it from Word and placing it into book design software, so that much of the formatting you laboriously created will be redone anyway.

Most printers require PDF files formatted to specific page size specifications. Creating these files requires considerable skill in using complex software programs like Adobe InDesign or QuarkXPress. These programs can take years to learn. If you're not experienced at working with them, your best bet is to hire a book designer to prepare your files.

However, even with formatting and embedded images, the effort the author has put into the book is not wasted. This draft manuscript can be a visual guide for what you wish your book to look like. Keep in mind, however, that Word is a very limited program for book design. Design software can do a far better job, so asking a designer to simply reproduce a Word book is limiting the outcome.

When submitting your Word text to a book designer, the only things you need to format are headings, bold or italic words, and chapter breaks.

The best way to deal with the placement of illustrations is to skip a line, and then write the file name of the image where you would like it to be. Often, it is best to leave the rest to your book designer, who will know of more sophisticated fonts, page layouts, and other attractive book features not available in Word.

If You are Not a Writer

You don't have to write to be an author. You don't even need a computer! If writing is not a practiced skill that you enjoy, then the labor of writing can inhibit you and slow you down.

Instead, tell your stories into a recorder, just as you would tell them face to face with another person. If you can, invite that other person to listen. You're more likely to relate your stories in vivid, full detail.

The stories you tell will probably be better, too. We are all born storytellers. Children learn the nuances of narrative simply by listening to stories. Before children learn actual words, they grasp the tone and intonation proper to different stories and imitate that speech pattern in babbling or nonsense syllables. Even before they attend school, children acquire a sense of story sequence, recognizing the importance of beginning a tale with the familiar words of "once upon a time" and bringing closure to a narrative with the words "the end." It is hard-wired into our brains to tell stories well.

Audio recording is also faster than writing. Imagine, a total of 4 hours of talking, at a normal pace, can produce a 100 page book! Your challenge will be to stay focused, since you will generate material so quickly.

Digital Recording

Oral historians have been gathering stories by recording for many years. Modern authors often dictate their books directly into the computer without typing. And you may even have precious cassettes of family members that you recorded years ago. If you are currently researching you family history and interviewing relatives for stories, telephone recording makes it possible to gather material from far-flung sources.

How do you incorporate these diverse audio recordings into a book? First, be certain to convert any older, analog material such as cassette recordings into a digital format. Converting a cassette to a digital recording is easy. Cassette recorders and players have stereo output ports, and computers have stereo input ports. Connect them with an inexpensive 1/8" stereo cable. Any software capable of recording audio on your computer will work with the cassette player.

We recommend *Audacity*, an excellent audio recording software which is available for free download. You can hook up a set of headphones and dictate directly on to your computer while *Audacity* records you.

Another way to dictate into the computer is a software program called *Dragon Naturally Speaking*, which converts your speech to text. Unfortunately, this technology is not flawless. If you do decide to purchase this software, we offer this advice from long experience: edit the text immediately after recording. There is often an unintelligible gap between what you said and what was typed, and it is difficult to remember later what you meant to say. With practice and cautious, clear enunciation, *Dragon Naturally Speaking* can be a very helpful tool.

Fortunately, there are affordable transcription services that will accept your digital recordings and type them up for you. Check your yellow pages for a local service, and do compare prices.

If you are gathering recordings from far-off sources, consider telephone recording. The technology depends on your equipment. There are analog devices that can be attached to your landline. Some people download Skype software, and call from the computer with compatible call recording software running in the background. Be aware that this method has limits if you are doing important archival recording. Because this is VOIP, (voice over the internet), your call recording quality can be subject to odd drop-outs.

Be sure to use a good telephone connection, and make sure your phone is working well. Do not record with a cell phone. Cell phones result in noisy, indecipherable recordings and dropped calls.

We have set up an extensive system that works wonderfully using the software *Trixbox*. Our callers can dial a toll-free number and are connected to a personal voice mailbox, where they can record an entire book's worth of stories. This requires a dedicated, always-on computer server, so it is appropriate only if you are gathering digital audio recordings on a larger scale, over time.

If you simply need to get one story from one distant person, consider buying an inexpensive hand-held digital recorder, purchased from a local office supply. They can mail it back to you once they've recorded, and you can then reuse it with your next interviewee.

Unfortunately, we have yet to find a digital reorder that is simple to operate. It is intimidating for someone to navigate those buttons, so expect some confusion and resistance. It is best to sit with your interviewee, and to operate the recorder yourself. For distant subjects, consider locating a tech-savvy young relative willing to sit with your interviewee and operate the recorder on your behalf.

How To Record Stories

Introduce your stories with the information from your Master Outline:

- The chapter number and working title.

- The story number and working title.

This information will help the transcriptionist, and can be removed later when the manuscript has been pieced together.

Speak clearly. Speak at your natural pace, but do not to slur your words. We recommend that you tell your story naturally, as you would to the audience of your book, as if you were gathered around the dinner table. Being informal makes you more expansive. (A glass of wine might help, as well.) You're more likely to use details, to provide those extra insights, if you're relaxed. You can also have a friend sit with you to be your "audience" – but remember to speak into the recorder. Don't let them talk, turning your story into a dialogue!

Some of our authors use notes to stay on track. A list of points you want to make can be handy. Most of our authors don't write out their stories; the quality is often better if you don't. It's up to you.

Note: If you have a speech disability or a heavy accent, there may be an extra step involved, yet audio recording is still possible. First, simply record your stories. Then have someone who understands you well and who can speak very clearly listen with a headset, and retell your stories into another recorder. It takes a little patience, but when your goal is to capture precious stories, it is certainly worth the effort to use this two-step process.

Spell out the name if your story has person or place with an uncommon name. Just spell it the first time you mention it. You will help your typist to be accurate and reduce the corrections to be made later.

When you have finished recording your story, you can listen to what you've recorded and decide whether to save it or delete it.

Interviewing Techniques

The situation: Say that you have decided to help a relative to record her memories. You've agreed upon a time to get together and you have a list of questions ready. Before you go, you might want to consider a few tips for interviewers like yourself, offered by the Regional Oral History Project at the University of California, Berkeley.

• Interviews usually work better if there is no one present but you and your relative.
• An interview is not a dialogue. The whole point is to get your relative to tell her story. Limit

your own remarks.
- Ask one question at a time.
- Ask brief questions.
- Start with questions that are not controversial; save the delicate questions (if there are any) for later in the interview.
- Don't let periods of silence fluster you. Give your relative a chance to think of what she wants to add before you hustle her along to the next question.
- Don't interrupt a good story because you have thought of a question, or because your relative is straying from your outline.
- End the interview at a reasonable time. An hour and a half is probably the maximum.

Tracking Your Progress

Your Master Outline has a checklist in the right-hand column. Use it to check off the stories you have written or told or gathered from others, and to plan for those still to be recorded. You can record your stories in any order you like. That's why it is so important that you identify the chapter and story title – you can sort and put them into order later.

Preparing Your Photos and Images

The ideal illustrated book is filled with colorful images. Full-color commercial printing service can reproduce color photographs and documents with wonderful, accurate color. Black and white photos look great, too. This is an amazing breakthrough in book printing technology – not too many years ago, a full-color book would have cost a fortune!

Handling Photo Prints

A photo binder is a useful method for sorting your photos and documents and for mailing them off to your book designer. Purchase a large three ring binder from an office supply and fill it with clear protective sleeves. Get the sleeves made from archival-quality materials, intended for the protection of photographs and other precious documents.

Each sleeve should hold two photographs. Place them back to back, so that the print's surface faces out, away from the other print. Slide them into the sleeve together gently.

This method allows you to leaf through and view images, and to rearrange them by swapping page inserts without touching or damaging the prints.

Preventing Physical Damage to Photographs

These guidelines are courtesy of Polaroid.com. The same rules apply to documents.

To preserve photographic images in the best possible condition, observe the following rules:

- Avoid writing on prints. If writing is necessary, do not write within the image area on the back of a print. Write in the border area with a soft pencil.

- Avoid bending, flexing or kinking photographs.

- Avoid paper clips, which can scratch the surface and leave an impression on the photograph or on adjacent photographs..

- Do not put staples through photographs. If you must use staples, place a staple across each of the four corners at an angle, without piercing the photograph.

- Use separating sheets of a suitable material between stapled photographs to prevent the possible scratching of prints. (Caution: Staples will rust, especially at relatively high humidity, and will damage the photographs.)

- Store photographs in such a way that they are not subjected to excessive pressure. When you mail photographs, be sure they are securely protected by stiff card stock to prevent accidental bending. Avoid abrasion. Slide photos carefully into or out of the envelopes made from rough materials.

- When sorting photographs in bulk, place a protective separating sheet of a suitable soft paper (such as archival tissue paper) between all pictures.

Assuring the Quality of Images

If you have some or all of your images as digital files already, that's great. Check your digital photos for quality, as you would a print. The file's resolution, or PPI (pixels per inch) must be at least 300 PPI, preferably higher.

Most common image file types are acceptable: .jpg, .psd, .tiff, .eps, .psd. However, .bmp and .gif files will not print at a high enough quality.

Image Scanning

We recommend using a flatbed scanner rather than a sheet-feed scanner because some sheet-fed scanners can cause artifacts in photos. Sheet scanners can also stress delicate materials.

Scanning at 300 dpi is a minimum acceptable level but 600 ppi is generally better for photo scans. For very small images that must be enlarged, scan at an even higher PPI. Unfortunately, if you are scanning poor quality photos, a higher PPI setting isn't going to make a difference.

Flatbed scanners with transparency adapters will generally work for scanning slides and negatives. Because scanning negatives and slides involves enlarging a tiny image, dust can become a big problem. You don't want to actually touch the negative or slide, but you can remove dust using a can of compressed air. You'll also want to clean off the scanner bed each time you scan to avoid dust as well. Compressed air will work here as well, but dust wipes are also very effective.

When performing the actual scanning, the software included with your scanner may be your best option. You'll want to select specifically what you're scanning, as you're not necessarily looking to scan the negative but rather the positive reproduction of the negative.

Photo Corrections

If you're not skilled in Photoshop, a book designer will perform all the basic adjustments to make your images look good: we adjust the color and contrast, eliminate red-eye, and in some cases, crop the picture to focus on the subject. But what if some of your photos are less than perfect? First, hunt around for the original negative. It will probably be in better condition than the print.

If a photo is special, you may choose to include it anyway. Consider repairing the damaged photo to make the image as clear as possible. There are two ways to do this:

Photo Restoration

A professional applies chemical treatments to alter the print. This can be expensive, and is generally reserved for very valuable photos. We recommend you locate a professional locally. Be sure to keep duplicates of the digital files once these rare treasures have been restored.

Photo Retouching

The digital image is manipulated using computer software. Photoshop has a variety of tools to adjust or alter flaws in an image. If any of your photos obviously needs to be touched up, indicate these photos to your scanning service or book designer.

PART 4
EDIT

Book Construction

Congratulations! You're well on your way towards a completed book. You've completed the first three steps of our 6-step process, Imagine, Plan, and Create. These steps were focused on the content to put into the book.

The next three steps will be the final construction of the book. Fortunately for you, most of this is our work, not yours. You'll give your editor and book designer some direction about your choices, and we'll do the rest. Here is an overview of your more supervisory role as you work with book specialists.

Step 4 Edit

Read though your manuscript. Confer with your editor and if you wish, ask for recommendations. Direct your editor to make revisions and corrections to the draft. Rename the chapter and story titles you wish to convert from working titles

Step 5 Design

Examine your scanned photos and documents to make final selections and place them in the book. Plan and write or record the captions to accompany your photos. Confer with your book designer about your printer/publisher choice, and then choose your preferences for the cover design, including photography, color scheme, text, typeface.

Step 6 Publish

Receive a final proof manuscript to check over for any final corrections. Examine the cover design for any final corrections. Authorize the final manuscript to be sent to the printer or publisher of your choice. Decide whether to order additional copies or to have books distributed.

Editing the Manuscript

So, now your stories are on paper, if not quite a book yet. The rough draft should be double-spaced, which makes it seem longer than your finished book will actually be. This draft contains only the text, so it will change again when we add the images later.

To get a sense of how long your book will be, we need three pieces of information:

- A word count, which can be found by selecting all your text in Word and choosing "Word Count" under the "Tools" menu.

- The size of the final book. You probably have an image of your final book in mind. This is a good time to explore what printer or publisher can create that size book for you.

- The number of images.

These three variables make it difficult to know exactly how long your book will be until its final layout with the book designer, but it is good to estimate now, so that you can get fair price estimates from printers and publishers.

Reading Your Rough Draft

We'll guide you with a systematic approach that will help you, and your editor, to improve the draft most logically, efficiently and effectively.

You should read though your draft at least two times. The first reading is a "macro" reading, where you consider the big picture. How effective is your book, as a whole? The second time is a "micro" reading, one that focuses on details and correctness. Since these are entirely different analytical processes, they should be done separately, and only in this order. Authors are inevitably emotional about their creative work, so we try to provide the dispassionate, logical approach you'll need.

Macro Reading

☐ The overall structure of the book, including sections, chapters, and sub-sections

☐ The content of the chapters and stories, and the content's place in the book

☐ The length and proportion of the chapters and stories

☐ Parts that are missing (stories, or details that must be added to stories)

☐ Parts that are not successful and should be cut out

Micro Reading

☐ Undesirable / unintended words and phrases

☐ Errors in content, such as facts that are incorrect

☐ Choices of wording, inaccuracies of word meanings

☐ Errors in spelling or punctuation

Why do a macro reading before a micro reading?

- Micro reading is very narrow and critical; it destroys your authentic first impression of the stories.

- Macro decisions will alter the book far more; they're more important.

- Macro decisions determine which parts of the book remain for a micro reading.

Your First, "Macro" Reading

Refer to the following Draft Revision Chart as you work with your rough draft manuscript. The purpose of this chart is to create a central document that tracks each desired change, rather than notes scattered in the margins of the draft.

Use this completed chart to confer with your editor and to discuss each change you want in a systematic way.

Your manuscript should have each line of text numbered. This makes it easy to locate any point in the text. Read the manuscript from the beginning, only considering the macro issues listed on the previous page. Use the Draft Revision Chart left columns to note the location (page, line#). Then identify the type of change you'd like to make.

All revisions fall into one of these categories: Add, Cut, Move, Revise, Correct. If you want to add just a few words, jot them down now. If you want to "Add" a lot more content, make a note to write or record later. "Revise" may also require returning to writing or recording if you're changing more than a sentence or two.

Resist the temptation to be distracted by minor errors; you'll deal with them later. Refer to the list of macro issues shown on the previous page to evaluate how you feel about the elements of your book.

If you find this process difficult, put the draft aside for a few days. Go back to your initial plans for the book, and reaffirm the reasons why you chose the stories you did. Then try again. You'll have plenty of feedback, support and advice when you have your conference with your editor. Save your Revision Chart and notes for the conference.

Page #	Line #	ADD	CUT	MOVE	REVISE	CORRECT	Changes Required	Completed
17	12	☒	☐	☐	☐	☐	"In Townsend, Texas, " (after we lived...)	☐
22	16	☐	☐	☐	☒	☐	I'll record another explanation to replace lines 16-96	☐
25	3	☐	☐	☐	☐	☒	Spelling is "Eleanore"	☐
34	1	☐	☐	☒	☐	☐	Move this story (pg 34-37) after Chapter 5, story 2 (see pg 48)	☐
41	10-16	☐	☒	☐	☐	☐		☐
		☐	☐	☐	☐	☐		☐
		☐	☐	☐	☐	☐		☐
		☐	☐	☐	☐	☐		☐
		☐	☐	☐	☐	☐		☐
		☐	☐	☐	☐	☐		☐
		☐	☐	☐	☐	☐		☐
		☐	☐	☐	☐	☐		☐
		☐	☐	☐	☐	☐		☐
		☐	☐	☐	☐	☐		☐

Your Second Reading

Your second reading depends upon your reaction to the book the first time you read it. Many of our authors are thrilled and proud and have created just the draft they expected. They make a few minor adjustments and are ready to move on.

However, you may not be so fortunate. Perhaps you didn't like the book very much on the first read. Perhaps you had many sections that you thought were seriously flawed, by the criteria in the list above. If so, **wait a few days before reading the draft again.** Put it and your notes aside.

It's better to tackle the draft with a fresh, emotionally distanced outlook. Before you read your draft again, go back to your initial notes and plans for the book, and reaffirm all the reasons why you chose the stories you did.

Then start the macro reading process again, as if you hadn't done it before. You may have a very different perception of it this time. Take notes again, on a fresh blank First Draft Revision Chart or piece of paper. Be nice to yourself.

It may reassure you to know that your editor has also read your book. He or she is experienced at this. If you think your book needs serious revisions, you'll have plenty of feedback, support and advice when you have your conference with your editor. Save your Revision Chart and notes for the conference.

Micro Reading

For your micro reading, you're fine-tuning the book. This requires a different kind of thinking. Do this in short sessions. If you look at the list of errors you want to correct in the list of "micro" issues on the previous page, they're all small errors - that's how they got into the book in the first place! Do this in short sessions, when you're fresh. When you get tired, you miss them.

In fact, most of these errors are so small they can be corrected right on the page where the error occurs. (That's why the draft is double spaced.) Circle the line number where the error occurred; write your correction in the margin or the space above it. Then fold down the corner of the page to indicate there is a correction on that page.

If you want to rewrite a sentence or two and don't have enough room on the draft, use the same method you used in the first reading, by writing on the Draft Revision Chart. Or you can write or type your new sentence on a separate sheet of paper. Then tuck the paper into the draft, right where the error occurred.

Why? It is easier to pass these changes on to your editor, or make the changes yourself. Using those dog-eared page corners, you can quickly flip to the page and line number for each correction. You can bypass the pages with their corners intact, knowing they don't have errors.

This kind of close reading can be a little daunting. Unfortunately, no editor or transcriptionist would know the correct spelling of a family member's name, for instance. Only you can give the draft a complete check for accuracy.

Some errors occur because the typist doesn't see the words you say, he only hears them. Occasionally you will find a string of question marks – this indicates that the recording of your voice wasn't clear, and the typist wants you to fill in the missing words.

Don't worry about missing an error or two. Your book will be read again and again by your editor, and you'll have a final version to proof read before it goes to the printer.

Working With Your Editor

Our authors say that the editorial conference is one of the highlights of their experience with creating a book. It's one thing to tell your family and friends about your project. It's another to talk it over with an experienced editor who has assembled, read, and edited your book.

When you are ready, after you have macro and micro read over the draft, schedule an appointment with your editor. Allow at least an hour for the session if you have significant changes you want to make to your book. Prepare for the meeting by looking over your draft, your Draft Revision Chart, and any additional notes you made. Keep an open mind; you may find that your mind has changed. That's all right.

Your editor will begin with the "macro" or content issues that you would like to change. You will go through the book in order, using the page numbers and line numbers you noted on your Draft Revision Chart.

If you want advice on how to improve your book, ask your editor for opinions and recommendations. You will get excellent guidance, and probably some very reassuring feedback. Not everyone seeks constructive criticism or wants to analyze their book. If you are happy with your book and don't request a critique, you won't get any unsolicited advice.

After the "macro" discussion, you and your editor will "flip through" the book, correcting the minor errors. We need your help in this, because there are some errors, such as correct names, that only you would recognize.

The Difference Between Revision and Editing

If you think about the word "re-vision", it literally means "to see again". Revising a draft is to see the very construction of the book again, to examine the "big picture".

A conference with your editor is your opportunity to revise: to add or delete or rearrange big chunks of the book. Your goal, and your editor's goal, is to arrive at an agreed-upon, satisfactory final form for the book. Your editor will make whatever changes you request.

In contrast, the editing is the "micro" aspect of your book. Small changes to sentences or individual words can be made to the final draft, if you miss something this time.

Once you've finished with the revison process, your editor will do a copyedit to make the samll corrections and you can move on to the design of the book. The next time you see your manuscript, it will be beautiful. Your pictures and documents will be placed throughout, you will see the colorful cover design, and it will have taken its final shape.

At that stage, you cannot "revise". The text and photos have been laboriously placed, just so, into a graphic design format. The text can't be moved around so easily. If we try to move more than just one paragraph, every other page shifts – what a mess! So we try not to revise again, although we can still edit at the word level.

Here is the best advice any author could have: after your editorial conference, once you have made the decisions and your editor has made the revisions to your rough draft, *don't look back*. Whatever choices you make: to add, to delete, to rearrange – make them once with your best judgment, then move on to completing the book. If you must, you can second guess your book - but don't third-guess. Nothing is perfect, and some people get trapped in this loop and never complete their book. If you are working with an editor, ask the editor if you are "done." If the answer is yes, stop revising. Just enjoy the book as it is and move on to finish it!

Better Chapter and Story Titles

When you've revised your manuscript and know the final outline of your book, you may wish to revisit your titles. Use a new, blank Master Outline form, but this time fill in any title you like.

Are chapter titles really necessary? No. How about story titles? No. Many successful books have "Chapter 1, Chapter 2, …" etc. You can start each story without any title at all. Or you can simply keep the working titles you've used so far.

Why are titles considered so important? When you decided how to organize your content into chapters, a lot of careful thought went into the process. You created a blueprint, a road map, a plan for how to get through your stories. Chapter titles that reveal your plan to your readers will help them follow your thinking more easily. They can see and admire your plan, in addition to enjoying the stories.

The one title you certainly can't evade is the title of your book. If all else fails you can always title it, "The Life and Times of … Your Name Here". Consider creating a unique title that reflects exactly the book you've written.

Types of Titles

Summary:	My Three Careers
Striking Statement:	I Landed at Normandy
Narrative:	Living the Summer of Love
Humorous:	The Four Year Program Took Me Nine Years
Question:	Remember the Rose Bowl?
Direct Address:	It Ain't What You Know, It's Who You Know

Story titles are even more suggestive. They encourage the reader to imagine in advance what the meaning of the story will be. They are a statement by the author that there is a hidden meaning in the story. It's a mystery the author has created, to be solved by the reader.

Good and Bad Titles

A clear title is easier for the reader. Depending on your audience, you may want to make it easier for them to understand you chapter by stating very directly what it's about.

- An obscure or enigmatic title may seem clever, but it may leave some people out.

- A dramatic title is memorable and appeals to the emotions. It will arouse curiosity and interest in the stories that follow.

- A title should be fitting; it should match the story that follows it.

- Unusual or unpronounceable words can be intimidating to readers.

- A title from a proverb or an old saying can weaken your story's effect. A cliché tells your reader what conclusion he should draw, before he's read the story.

- A title for the whole work is meant to unify its elements – stories, chapters and ideas. It can make a statement about how they are related.

PART 5
DESIGN

Book Interior Design

Once you know the final shape of your book's text, you can make decisions about placing and captioning your images. You don't have to use every one of the photos you originally selected. Sort through them with a critical eye.

If you have submitted your images to a book designer, you can refer to the contact sheets he or she will provide to you. Contact sheets have "thumbnail" miniatures of your scanned photos and documents. (Use the original photographs if you'd like to study the full-size images.) These reproductions of your photographs are used to give you an overview of the scans, corrections, and crops already done on your images. The colors of the contact sheets are not altogether accurate, as an office printer can't match the commercial printer they've been prepared for. Don't worry if their colors are "off" -they'll look great in your book.

Using the Photo Placement Chart

Begin by eliminating photos. Mark an "X" next to the photo number in the second column of the Photo Chart, "Do Not Use".

Placing Photos and Documents

Some of your photos may perfectly illustrate a given story. Those are usually the first to be "assigned" to a place in the book. Write the chapter number on the Photo Chart. If there is a specific story in that chapter that the image corresponds to, write the story number as well.

Featured Photos

Next, use the contact sheets to single out your favorites. Choose 10 to 15 photos that you think are excellent - your "featured photos". From them, choose the best photos for your book's front and back covers. The others can be displayed on a single, full page (or significantly enlarged, if the photo is too small). Indicate the photos you select for the covers and for "featured" placement on the Photo Chart.

Front Cover Image(s)_____   Front Flap Image _____

Back Cover Image(s)_____   Back Flap Image _____

Photo	Do NOT place in book? Mark with "X"	Featured Image? Mark with ✓	Place in book Chapter	Story	Place in group? List other photo #'s	Caption? Mark with ✓
1						
2						
3						
4						
5						
6						
7						
8						
9						
10						
11						
12						
13						
14						

Not every image is, or must be, so literally connected to your stories. To include more loosely related photos, we can group them together, or place them singly, between chapters. To do this, find one or more photos you would like to place between chapters. On the Photo Chart write the numbers of the photos you want grouped together. In the Placement column specify where the photos should appear. Up to 12 photos can fit on a page in a group, but the more photos you put on a page, the smaller they will be. Instead of grouping 12 or 8 photos, you may want to make groups of just 2 or 4 per page. Photo collages are usually not recommended for more scholarly works such as a family history, as they are more difficult for the reader to comprehend.

Captioning Photos and Documents

Consider whether the image needs identification (who, what, when, where, why, how). Not every photo needs a caption, and documents often speak for themselves. Consider grouping pictures without captions in some sections of your book. It allows the reader to enjoy a purely visual, non-verbal experience, to break up the "wordiness" of reading stories. Self-explanatory photos, such as multiple images of the same person, are also better off without a caption.

Mark the Caption column with a check if you will caption the image. After you have considered all your images, create a new document or record your captions for transcription. In general, captions should be 20 words or fewer.

Table of Contents

Your table of contents may be more or less detailed, depending on your content. For books that list stories, a list of contents may be adequate. For more complex books, sections, chapters, subsections and even illustrations may be listed in the table of contents. This allows the reader to use the book more as a reference, rather than leafing through at random.

Cover Design

The cover of your book has special meaning. It is the first thing that others see, the part of the book that your readers will examine most closely. It is worth the effort to make it look great – something you can be very proud of. Because your cover is unique, your designer will consult with you as it is designed. There are many choices, including the colors, fonts, and layered designs, too many to reprint here. This section gives you an overview of the choices involved. However, if you prefer, you can also place these decisions in your designer's hands.

Cover Materials

You have a choice of cover materials. A hardcover with a dust jacket is a continuous sheet of high-gloss, heavy stock, full color paper, which is fitted around the hard cover of the book. Another hardcover, called "Imagewrap", does not have a dust jacket. The image is printed directly on to the cover in a plasticized material. Both styles of hardcover book are appropriate for long-lasting heirloom books. If quality is important to you, then a hard cover with a sewn binding is essential, although it will cost more per book.

Softcover books are available, too, and some authors order both to keep costs down. Because prices vary, and not every printer provides both, discuss this choice with your book designer. In any case, the goal is to artfully design the front, back, and spine, and the inner flaps if you choose the dust jacket option.

Photography

The first element of your cover is often the photograph or photographs you choose to feature. This image should be in excellent condition, because it will likely be reprinted at a large size and will be examined closely.

You can choose to use another photograph(s) on the back of the book, leave the back cover plain, or provide text for the back of the book. On books that have a dust jacket, it is common to have an author's photo and a brief bio. Commercial books often use this space for promotional blurbs, and that is possible to do even if you are printing privately.

Color Scheme

Generally, you will choose one dominant color for your book cover and one or two accent colora. If you choose to use a full-bleed (full size to the edge of the paper) photograph on the front and back cover, your color selection will be seen only on the spine and dust flaps, if any.

You can also choose a color that complements a dominant color in your featured photograph(s). For instance, if your photograph has a blue sky background, match that color with a complementary color for the rest of your book jacket.

Typefaces and Fonts

Your book cover is unique, and you will want to use stylish type that makes a statement. If you are a computer user, you can look at a wide variety of fonts available in Word, or you may even have Adobe fonts installed. Your book designers should have many fonts in stock. There are also many sites online with fonts, although if neither you nor your designer owns the font, you may have to pay for it.

Text

Your text color should be selected to contrast with your cover's background. You may wish to have text on the back cover, and in some cases on the dust jacket flaps. You may wish to give a summary of the book's contents, or a sample quotation from one of the stories, or both. Tradition-ally, a blurb about the author appears on the rear flap, limited to just a paragraph.

Additional Features

Do you have another element or image you would like to see on the cover of your book? If so, ask. You can use cover artwork other than photos. Your designer may have the image you are seeking in stock. Or your designer can research on the internet to purchase your perfect artwork.

The Final Proof

The final proof is your chance to look over the fully designed and formatted book before it goes to the printer. You will receive the final draft for proofreading after your designer has incorporated all your photos, captions, and cover design choices.

The final proof will be identical to your actual book in almost every respect. The content of each page is the same. The photos and text won't change. However, a designer cannot achieve the same color palette with an office printer as the commercial book printer's colors. We can checked your photos on a computer monitor calibrated to be identical to the printer's, so we've seen the true colors, we just can't print them. Please disregard any colors that seem a bit "off". To be absolutely certain that your book's colors will be perfect, arrange to order a copy from the printer or publisher before placing a large order.

The Book Cover Mockup

You will also receive two or three additional sheets that represent the cover design: the front, back, spine and flaps, depending on your choice of binding. The designer cannot print your actual dust jacket. Given the dimensions, only the commercial printer can roll out a sheet of that size and weight. But we can print a good approximation. Please be tolerant of any minor color variances and focus on the design elements themselves. Make sure you're happy with the photography and fonts, and double-check the text and any other elements.

Proofreading the Text for Errors

We encourage you to proofread the manuscript closely, again. Give it to a friend and ask them to give it a read, too. We're humble enough to admit that an editor might miss something, and it is better to find a flaw now, rather than later.

Unlike your rough draft, the final version doesn't have line numbers. This makes it a little more difficult to indicate the exact place an error is located on the page. We've found the easiest way to avoid any confusion is to note all changes you see and want made. Then call your editor and confer with him, so he can locate the exact place on the manuscript page with your help.

Final Approval

The Final Approval Form is an agreement that you usually receive from an editor, and definitely from a designer. It states that all changes have been made, that you're truly locked into this final version, and that your designer should go ahead and send your book to the printer. Triple - check your book. If it is possible, don't order extra copies until you receive your first book. When you've examined it and spent some time with it and again believe it is perfect, then invest in additional copies.

PART 6
PUBLISH

Understanding Self Publishing

When we talk with authors, most of them say, "I need to find a publisher for my book." In fact, they may not need a publisher at all. They are interested in what used to be referred to as *private publication,* where a small number of copies of their book will be printed for distribution to family and friends. What these authors really need is a printer, not a publisher. Understanding the difference between printing and publishing can save a self publishing author a lot of money.

Publishers are companies involved in both production and **commercial distribution** of a book. They are contracted with the writer from the development of the idea for the book through its writing, editing design, production and sales. They pay a writer an advance and royalties in exchange for the rights to shape and sell the book as they see fit.

What our self publishing clients are often really looking for is someone to **print** their book. If you are planning on only a handful of copies, commercial contracts, marketing and distribution aren't things you should be concerned about. Nor should you have to pay for distribution services. There are many on-demand printers and publishers to choose from. However, their prices and terms vary widely.

Many publishers package their printing services together with marketing services, a package that is designed for authors attempting to sell books. These fees are unnecessary for those authors who are self publishing for family and friends.

Publishers, both traditional publishers and digital self publishers like CreateSpace, XLibris, or iUniverse, sell you distribution services and take a profit from each book, whether you need these services or not. When considering a commercial print-on-demand service, be sure to ask these questions:

- Are you being charged extra fees for editing, proofreading, custom design, or book marketing that you do not need?

- Do you retain all rights to your book, including the files you submit and the ISBN?

- If your book is to be sold from their online bookstore, do you get all the proceeds, or do they charge a percentge?

- Can you take your book to a different publisher or printer and attempt to sell it elsewhere?

Digital and Offset Printers

If you deal with a printer you will pay only the cost of producing your book. You must prepare your manuscript to the printer's specifications. This often means employing the services of an editor and a book designer. But the printer - particularly on-demand printers - will take the files you submit and print exactly the number of copies you want. You will pay only the costs of printing. Authors can make choices that further control the cost of their book. Hardback or softcover? How many pages? Full color or black and white? Your editor or book designer can help you to locate the right mix, and the right printer for your project.

There are two types of printers – digital print on demand (POD) and offset printers. Digital printing has made it possible to print a single book, or a few, at a modest cost. The printer does not print a book until he receives an order for it. The price per book is a fixed manufacturing cost, with discounts for volume. The unit cost is somewhat higher with a digital book than with traditional offset printing. However, the average cost of the total order is dramatically lower for small print runs because there is no minimum order.

What is particularly desirable for a cost conscious author is that she can complete her book, submit it to a digital on-demand printer and let each family member or friend know that they can purchase their copy of the book directly from the printer in the online bookstore. Sites such as Blurb.com and Lulu.com make books available for purchase without an ISBN in their online bookstores. The author no longer faces the prospect of paying the entire cost of printing the book. Self-publishing makes it possible to distribute the printing costs among all of the intended recipients, so the author only bears the cost of editing and design services.

Offset printers often have setup fees and a print run minimum, making them more expensive than digital printers initially. However, their presses are capable of using higher quality inks, and many offset presses offer a variety of custom bindings. If you are looking for high-end printing and features like leather or embossed covers, consider an offset printer. Discuss the number of copies you need to see if this is economically feasible for you.

Commercial Options

An increasing number of authors are embracing self-publishing as a commercial proposition. An aspiring author who fails to find a deal with traditional publishers, or one who is unhappy with the terms offered by publishers, may opt to go it alone.

If you are planning to produce a memoir or family history book for commercial distribution, the services of companies like iUniverse, Create Space, Lulu, or Xlibris may look very attractive. But before you sign up you should consider all aspects of the service packages offered by these companies including:

- Who controls the rights to the book?

- What share of the sale price of each book goes to the company and what to the author?

- What are the limits of book distribution offered by these publishers?

- What marketing and publicity services are actually included in the service package?

- Does the package include personal services by a professional editor or book designer or a template based program?

There are some advantages to the services these companies offer. But authors thinking of using one should research exactly what they are buying before putting their names on a contract. If the book fails to thrive in the commercial market, it is good to keep your options open, as you may wish to try printing or publishing elsewhere.

Authors hoping to sell many copies will not wish to limit themselves to to just a few outlets and methods of distribution. The best deal around for commercial publishing is Lightning Source. If you're self publishing on a large scale and intend to write and sell more than one book, you may want to move from "author" to "publisher". Check out the book *POD for Profit* by Aaron Shepard, which describes how to maximize profits by printing your books through Lighting Source.

There are drawbacks for an author seeking commercial distribution of a self-published book. Two of the most important are that book stores may refuse to stock self-published works and reviewers may be unwilling to review them.

Why? Here is the typical industry response. "It's not that I have a philosophical objection to self-published books, but the reality is that most of them don't cleave to the same editorial or production standards as books that come from reputable publishing houses," says Steven Beattie, *Quill & Quire*'s review editor.

It is true, there are a lot of junky books out there, commercial and self published. We know yours is better than that. If you have commercial aspirations, hire a book doctor to give you an honest evaluation of your chances with traditional publishers. It is certainly easier to hand off your book to a good publisher, if they will successfully market it on your behalf, particularly if the publisher offers a substantial advance.

Finding a Printer

How do you find a good printer who is right for you? It is a great source of confusion that many printers are also publishers, offering both services. The printing business you seek may be named "John Doe Publishers."

When you contact such a business, you will need to clarify what you want, a simple print job or full publishing services. Ask which they offer and on what terms. Do not limit your search to local companies, as these companies are all online and exchange book files digitally.

Ask about the physical features of a book when selecting a printer or publisher. Some features that will help make your book a family heirloom are:

- Hard cover with a protective covering such as a dust jacket, plasticized Imagewrap or custom leatherette

- Quality binding; usually over-sewn or sewn through the fold rather than adhesive binding

- Full color printing

- Quality paper with enough weight to both retain the ink well and be opaque enough for two-sided printing of images

Printers and publishers vary in terms of the services they provide, including paper quality, type of cover, and number of images. As you work on your book, it is a great idea to investigate several potential publishers. Talk with them and determine early on who you want to work with. If you wait until you are finished with your book to talk with them, it may be too time consuming or costly to make the changes to get the book the way you really want it.

It is possible to save money on the cost per book by doing things like using paperback covers, glue bindings and limiting color in the book's interior. However, we always recommend that if you are printing a limited number of copies for family members you will be better served if you spend a few extra dollars for a higher quality book. After all, you expect your book to be passed on from generation to generation. That will only work with a book built to last.

If you plan to print a small number of books, make sure that your printer will retain your files and guarantee that future prints will be identical to the initial print run.

You might want to check out the recommendations of the Hardcover Binders International, a printing trade group, insuring quality, durability and longevity in a book.

Do I Need an ISBN or Copyright?

First, let's clarify exactly an ISBN is. An ISBN (International Standard Book Number) is the 13 digit number usually accompanied by a bar code on the book's back cover or the inside front cover of a mass market paperback. R.W. Bowker, the company which serves as the U.S. ISBN Agency says, "The purpose of the ISBN is to establish and identify one title or edition of a title from one specific publisher and is unique to that edition allowing more efficient marketing of products by booksellers, libraries, universities, wholesalers, and distributors." The fee is $275 for 10 ISBNs. (Single ISBNs can be obtained through publishers.) The fee for bar codes is $25 each for 1-5 bar codes, and your book will have the bar code placed on the cover for scanner identification.

If you are considering commercial distribution, you'll need an ISBN to offer the book in stores and online sites such as amazon.com. If you intend only a limited distribution to family and a few friends, you probably won't need to get one. A printer should not require you to purchase an ISBN. You can buy a batch of books and distribute them yourself without one. Some online print on demand bookstores, such as lulu.com and blurb.com, allow you to sell your book from their online bookstore without an ISBN. Amazon.com's CreateSpaces will issue an ISBN for free. The downside is that in exchange they become your publisher, and you cannot take the book elsewhere.

The US Copyright Office defines copyright as "a form of protection grounded in the U.S. Constitution… (it's) a form of intellectual property law which protects original forms of authorship." Work is under copyright at the moment it is created. Registration of a copyright is voluntary, but you must register if you bring a lawsuit for copyright infringement. The Copyright Office advises, "Many choose to register their works because they wish to have the facts of their copyright on the public record and have a certification of public record." Registration within five years of publication is considered *prima facie* evidence in a court. The basic fee to register a copyright online is $35.

If you are an historian and wish to place your work on the public record for other researchers, this will probably be enough.

What About Ebooks?

It has been fascinating to watch the rapid evolution of ebooks, both as a technological platform and as a publishing platform. As a consumer, you may have already purchased an ebook reader, such as Amazon's Kindle or the Nook from Barnes and Noble. Apple's entry into the field with the iPad is expected to result in an explosion of new titles available to readers in the ebook format. Yet the workings of this industry behind the scenes, where books are actually created for delivery to these devices, is still evolving.

The publishing of ebooks has upended and overturned the traditional model of commercial publishing. The traditional author worked through an agent, one who negotiated each book individually with publishing houses to determine the market value of a book. The author's rights to print, web, and film could be negotiated separately. If the deal didn't go through, the agent could shop the book around to other publishers.

The ebook market is far less flexible for the author. Because the producers of these devices control the publishing platform, they get to set the terms. At Amazon and Apple, the terms are set: a 70/30 split. The difference comes in book pricing. Apple will sell every book on its iPad for $9.99, an arbitrary price point the author cannot control. Amazon is willing to offer ebooks at a significantly lower price. Although the 70/30 split is a higher percentage than the author could get from a traditional publisher, these low ebook prices will net far less for the author than the proceeds from a trade paperback.

Recently, Barnes and Noble announced the creation of PubIt!, their new ebook publishing division. Whether they can offer more attractive terms for authors remains to be seen.

The stakes are higher than ever before. This isn't just an issue of the author's contract, whether he makes a few cents more or less per book. Because there are just a few giants in the ebook business, Apple, Amazon and Barnes & Noble don't just sell the reading devices, they also control the distribution of ebooks. You can't choose to shop at an independent bookstore down the street if you don't like what they're offering.

Is it a good idea to publish your book in ebook form? You are not likely to make a profit from a wide readership, but an ebook can be useful to your existing readers. The multimedia form can offer a more complex experience. You can incorporate video and audio into the book experience. One of the best features of ebooks is the embedded internet links, opening up more avenues of exploration for the reader.

However, ebooks are an ephemeral media, as is all digital media. The CD disk is fragile and may soon be obsolete. Do not entrust creative works to digital media alone; they can be lost forever. Books are still the only reliable archival media. And they are wonderful to hold, too.

Made in the USA
Charleston, SC
15 January 2011